FIRST 50
CLASSICAL PIECES
YOU SHOULD PLAY ON THE VIOLIN

ISBN 978-1-5400-2471-8

Visit Hal Leonard Online at
www.halleonard.com

Contact us:
Hal Leonard
7777 West Bluemound Road
Milwaukee, WI 53213
Email: info@halleonard.com

In Europe, contact:
Hal Leonard Europe Limited
42 Wigmore Street
Marylebone, London, W1U 2RN
Email: info@halleonardeurope.com

In Australia, contact:
Hal Leonard Australia Pty. Ltd.
4 Lentara Court
Cheltenham, Victoria, 3192 Australia
Email: info@halleonard.com.au

CONTENTS
BY TITLE

4 About Strange Lands and People ....Robert Schumann

6 Air from *Water Music* ....George Frideric Handel

9 Air on the G String ....J.S. Bach

16 Arioso ....J.S. Bach

12 Ave Maria.. Franz Schubert

19 Barcarolle from *The Tales of Hoffmann* .... Jacques Offenbach

24 Berceuse .... Benjamin Godard

25 The Blue Danube Waltz.................Johann Strauss II

28 Canon in D ....Johann Pachelbel

33 Caro mio ben .... Tommaso Giordani

36 Chanson Triste...................Pyotr Il'yich Tchaikovsky

38 Country Gardens......................English Morris Dance

40 Dance of the Blessed Spirits from *Orfeo ed Euridice* ....Christoph Willibald von Gluck

44 Dona Nobis Pacem ....Traditional

46 La donna è mobile............................ Giuseppe Verdi

48 Emperor Waltz.................................Johann Strauss II

52 Evening Prayer from *Hansel and Gretel* ....Engelbert Humperdinck

54 Gavotte .... François-Joseph Gossec

55 He Shall Feed His Flock from *Messiah* .... George Frideric Handel

58 Hungarian Dance No. 5.................Johannes Brahms

62 Jupiter Chorale from *The Planets* ......Gustav Holst

64 Largo from *Serse* .... George Frideric Handel

66 Largo from Symphony No. 9 "From the New World".................... Antonín Dvořák

61 Lullaby (Wiegenlied)....................Johannes Brahms

68 The Merry Farmer .... Robert Schumann

70 The Merry Widow Waltz .... Franz Lehár

72 Minuet..................................... Ignacy Jan Paderewski

74 Minuet in G Major.................Ludwig van Beethoven

78 Minuet in G Major, BWV Anh. 114 ....Christian Petzold

80 Minuet in G Minor, BWV Anh. 115 ....Christian Petzold

75 The Moldau .... Bedřich Smetana

82 Musetta's Waltz (Quando men vo) from *La Bohème*..............................Giacomo Puccini

88 Nel cor più non mi sento............. Giovanni Paisiello

85 O mio babbino caro from *Gianni Schicchi* ....Giacomo Puccini

90 Ode to Joy ....Ludwig van Beethoven

92 Pavane .... Gabriel Fauré

94 Les Plaisirs ....George Philipp Telemann

96 Pomp and Circumstance..................... Edward Elgar

98 Romance from *Eine kleine Nachtmusik* .... Wolfgang Amadeus Mozart

102 Sheep May Safely Graze.............................J.S. Bach

99 The Skaters' Waltz.........................Émile Waldteufel

106 The Sleeping Beauty Waltz .... Pyotr Il'yich Tchaikovsky

105 Surprise Symphony (Second Movement Theme) ....Joseph Haydn

110 Swan Lake (Theme) ....Pyotr Il'yich Tchaikovsky

114 Symphony No. 1 (Fourth Movement Theme) ....Johannes Brahms

116 To a Wild Rose ....Edward MacDowell

118 To Music (An die Musik)................... Franz Schubert

120 Waltz, Op. 39, No. 15 ....Johannes Brahms

122 Watchman's Song ....Edvard Grieg

126 Winter from *The Four Seasons* (Second Movement) .... Antonio Vivaldi

The pieces in this book have been arranged and transcribed from their original instrumentation by Celeste Avery, Martin Hodges, John Reed, and Christopher Ruck.

CONTENTS
BY COMPOSER

JOHANN SEBASTIAN BACH
9   Air on the G String
16   Arioso
102   Sheep May Safely Graze

LUDWIG VAN BEETHOVEN
74   Minuet in G Major
90   Ode to Joy

JOHANNES BRAHMS
58   Hungarian Dance No. 5
61   Lullaby (Wiegenlied)
114   Symphony No. 1 (Fourth Movement Theme)
120   Waltz, Op. 39, No. 15

ANTONÍN DVOŘÁK
66   Largo from *The New World Symphony*

EDWARD ELGAR
96   Pomp and Circumstance

GABRIEL FAURÉ
92   Pavane

TOMMASO GIORDANI
33   Caro mio ben

CHRISTOPH WILLIBALD VON GLUCK
40   Dance of the Blessed Spirits
      from *Orfeo ed Euridice*

JACQUES OFFENBACH
19   Barcarolle from *The Tales of Hoffmann*

JOHANN PACHLEBEL
28   Canon in D

IGNACY JAN PADAREWSKI
72   Minuet

GIOVANNI PAISIELLO
88   Nel cor più non mi sento

CHRISTIAN PETZOLD
78   Minuet in G Major, BWV Anh. 114
80   Minuet in G Minor, BWV Anh. 115

GIACOMO PUCCINI
82   Musetta's Waltz (Quando men vo)
      from *La Bohème*
85   O mio babbino caro from *Gianni Schicchi*

FRANZ SCHUBERT
12   Ave Maria
118   To Music (An die Musik)

ROBERT SCHUMANN
4   About Strange Lands and People
68   The Merry Farmer

BEDŘICH SMETANA

About Strange Lands and People

from *Kinderszenen (Scenes from Childhood)*, Op. 15, No. 1

originally for piano

Robert Schumann
(1810–1856)

Air
from *Water Music*
originally for Baroque orchestra

George Frideric Handel
(1685–1759)

Slowly and stately

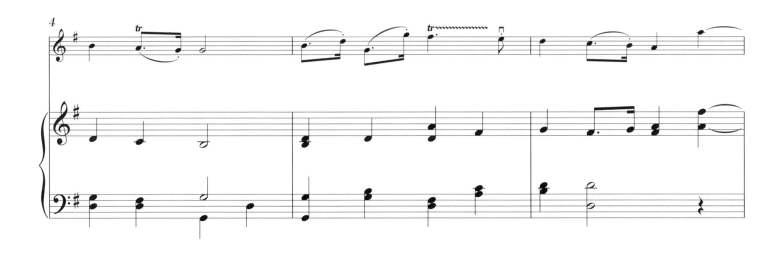

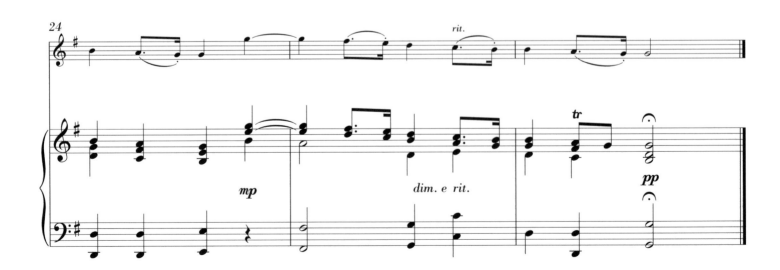

Air

(Air on the G String)
from Orchestral Suite No. 3 in D Major, BWV 1068

Johann Sebastian Bach
(1685–1750)

Ave Maria

originally for voice and piano

Franz Schubert
(1797–1828)

Arioso
(Sinfonia)
from Cantata, BWV 156

originally for Baroque orchestra

Johann Sebastian Bach
(1685–1750)

Barcarolle
from the opera *The Tales of Hoffmann*

Jacques Offenbach
(1819–1880)

Berceuse
from *Jocelyn*
originally for orchestra

Benjamin Godard
(1849–1895)

The Blue Danube Waltz

originally for orchestra

Johann Strauss II
(1825-1899)

Canon in D

originally for Baroque orchestra

Johann Pachelbel
(1653-1706)

Caro mio ben

originally for voice and piano

Tommaso Giordani
(1730–1806)

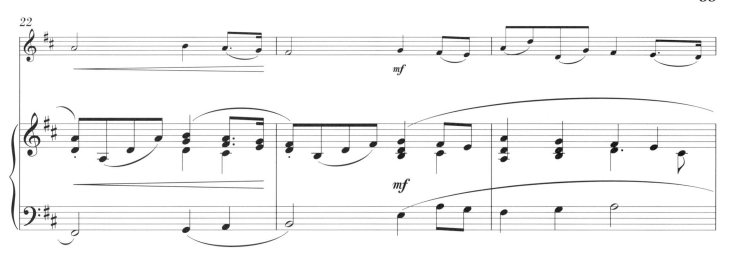

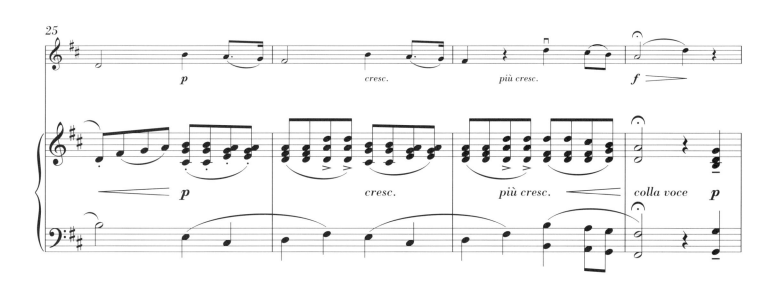

Chanson Triste
from *Douze Morceaux*, Op. 40, No. 2
originally for piano

Pyotr Il'yich Tchaikovsky
(1840–1893)

Country Gardens

English Morris Dance

Dance of the Blessed Spirits

from *Orfeo ed Euridice*

originally for orchestra

Christoph Willibald von Gluck
(1714–1787)

This page has been intentionally left blank to facilitate page turns.

Dona Nobis Pacem

originally for chorus

Traditional

La donna è mobile

from the opera *Rigoletto*

Giuseppe Verdi
(1813–1901)

Emperor Waltz

originally for orchestra

Johann Strauss II
(1825–1899)

Evening Prayer

from the opera *Hansel and Gretel*

Engelbert Humperdinck
(1854–1921)

Gavotte

originally for piano

François-Joseph Gossec
(1734–1829)

He Shall Feed His Flock

from the oratorio *Messiah*

George Frideric Handel
(1685–1759)

Hungarian Dance No. 5

originally for piano

Transcribed by Christopher Ruck

Johannes Brahms
(1833-1897)

Lullaby
(Wiegenlied)

originally for voice and piano

Johannes Brahms
(1833-1897)

Jupiter Chorale

from *The Planets*

originally for orchestra

Gustav Holst
(1874–1934)

Largo

(Ombra mai fù)

from the opera *Serse*, HWV 40

George Frideric Handel
(1685–1759)

Largo

from Symphony No. 9 "From the New World"

originally for orchestra

Antonín Dvořák
(1841–1904)

The Merry Farmer

from *Album for the Young*, Op. 68, No. 10

originally for piano

Robert Schumann
(1810–1856)

Brisk and Lively

The Merry Widow Waltz

from the opera *The Merry Widow*

Franz Lehár
(1870–1948)

Valse moderato

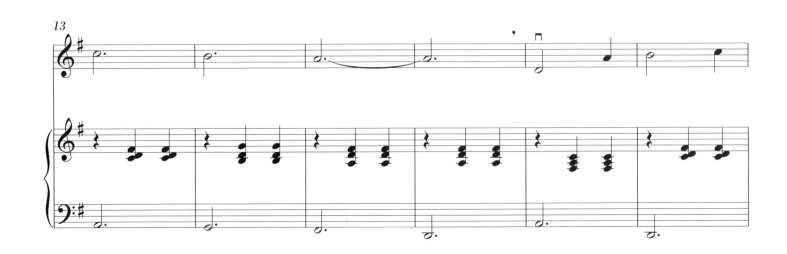

Minuet

originally for piano

Ignacy Jan Padarewski
(1860-1941)

Minuet in G
WoO 10, No. 2
originally for piano

Ludwig van Beethoven
(1770-1827)

The Moldau
from *Ma Vlast*
originally for orchestra

Bedřich Smetana
(1824-1884)

Minuet in G Major
BWV Anh. 114
from *Notebook for Anna Magdalena Bach*
originally for keyboard

Christian Petzold
(1677–1733)

Minuet in G Minor

BWV Anh. 115

from *Notebook for Anna Magdalena Bach*

originally for keyboard

Christian Petzold
(1677–1733)

Musetta's Waltz
(Quando men vo)
from the opera *La Bohème*

Giacomo Puccini
(1858–1924)

O mio babbino caro

from the opera *Gianni Schicchi*

Giacomo Puccini
(1858-1924)

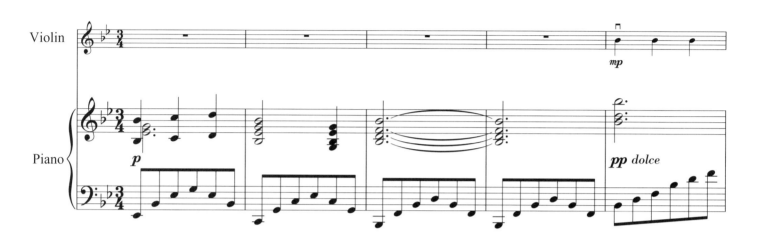

Nel cor più non mi sento

from the opera *L'amor contrastato*

Giovanni Paisiello
(1740–1816)

Ode to Joy

from Symphony No. 9

originally for orchestra

Ludwig van Beethoven
(1770-1827)

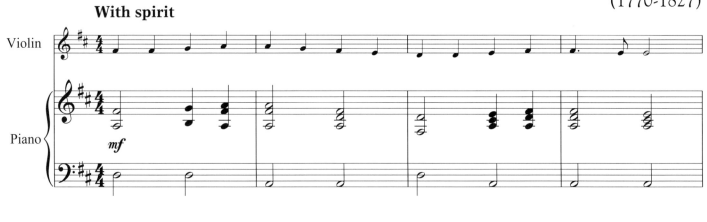

Pavane

originally for orchestra

Gabriel Fauré
(1845–1924)

Les Plaisirs
(The Pleasures)
from the *Suite for Recorder and Strings in A minor*, TV 55, No. 12
originally for Baroque orchestra

Georg Philipp Telemann
(1681–1767)

Pomp and Circumstance
March No. 1
originally for orchestra

Edward Elgar
(1857-1934)

Romance
from *Eine kleine Nachtmusik (A Little Night Music)*
originally for orchestra

Wolfgang Amadeus Mozart
(1756-1791)

The Skaters' Waltz

originally for orchestra

Émile Waldteufel
(1837–1915)

Sheep May Safely Graze

from the cantata *The lively hunt is my heart's desire!*
(Was mir behagt, ist nur die muntre Jagd!), BWV 208

originally for chorus and Baroque orchestra

Johann Sebastian Bach
(1685–1750)

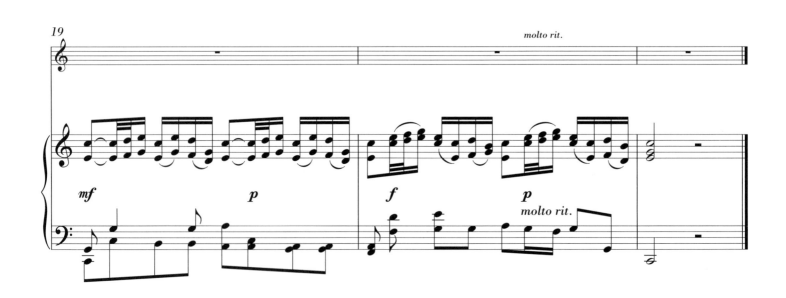

Surprise Symphony
(Second Movement Theme)

originally for orchestra

Joseph Haydn
(1732-1809)

The Sleeping Beauty Waltz

from the ballet *The Sleeping Beauty*

originally for orchestra

Pyotr Il'yich Tchaikovsky
(1840–1893)

Swan Lake
(Theme from the ballet)

originally for orchestra

Pyotr Il'yich Tchaikovsky
(1840–1893)

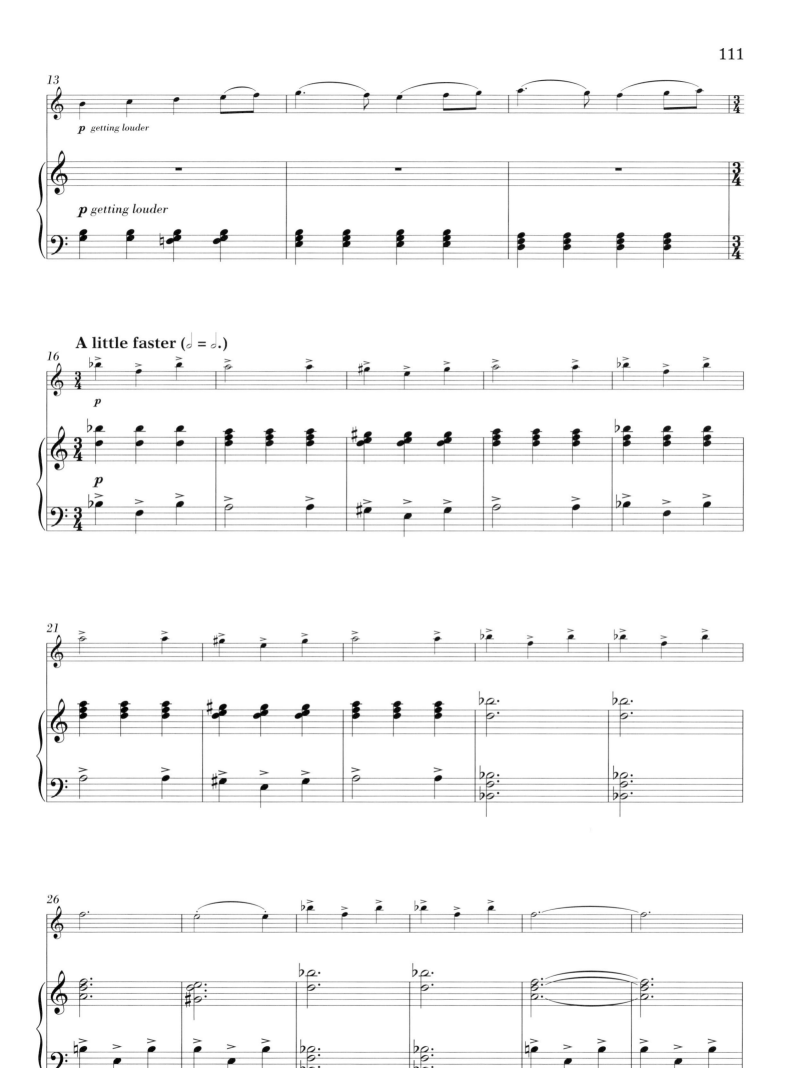

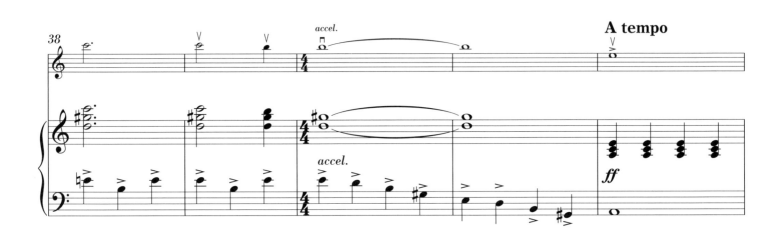

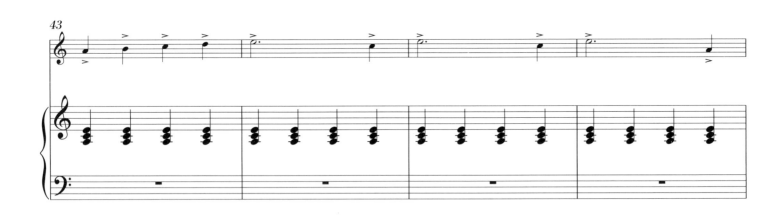

This page has been intentionally left blank to facilitate page turns.

Symphony No. 1
(Fourth Movement Theme)
originally for orchestra

Johannes Brahms
(1833-1897)

To a Wild Rose

from *Woodland Sketches*, Op. 51, No. 1

originally for piano

Edward MacDowell
(1860–1908)

To Music
(An die Musik)
originally for voice and piano

Franz Schubert
(1797–1828)

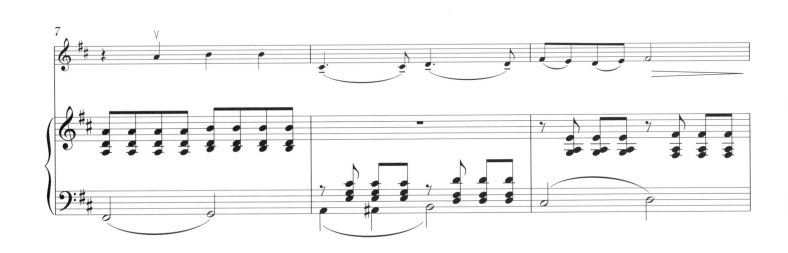

Waltz
Op. 39, No. 15
originally for piano

Johannes Brahms
(1833–1897)

Watchman's Song

from *Lyric Pieces*, Op. 12, No. 3

originally for piano

Edvard Grieg
(1843–1907)

Intermezzo
Spirits of Night

Winter
(Second Movement)
from *The Four Seasons*
originally for Baroque orchestra

Antonio Vivaldi
(1678–1741)